CHALLENGE
YOURSELF

AMAZING PLACES

WEIRD TRIVIA AND UNBELIEVABLE FACTS TO TEST YOUR KNOWLEDGE
ABOUT THE MOST EXTREME PLACES ON EARTH!

JEFF PROBST

CHALLENGE YOURSELF

AMAZING PLACES

YOURSELF

Puffin Books
An Imprint of Penguin Group (USA)

PUFFIN BOOKS
Published by the Penguin Group
Penguin Group (USA) LLC
375 Hudson Street
New York, New York 10014

USA * Canada * UK * Ireland * Australia
New Zealand * India * South Africa * China

penguin.com
A Penguin Random House Company

First published in the United States of America by Puffin Books,
an imprint of Penguin Young Readers Group, 2015

LIBRARY OF CONGRESS CATALOGING-IN-PUBLICATION DATA IS AVAILABLE

Puffin Books Hardcover ISBN 978-0-14-751617-6
Paperback ISBN 978-0-14-751376-2

Printed in China

1 3 5 7 9 10 8 6 4 2

Designed by Maria Fazio

Photo Credits

Thinkstock: Pages i, vi, 2, 5, 8,-10, 12, 16, 17-18, 20, 22, 25, 27-29, 31-32, 34, 37-39, 42-44,
46, 50-52, 54-55, 57-58, 68-73, 79-80, 82-87, 89-96, 98, 101-102, 106, 109-110, 114, 116-118,
121-122, 125-127, 130, 132134, 137-138, 140, 142, 145, 150-151,153, 155, 159

Shutterstock: Pages ii, 5-8, 15,17, 21, 24-25, 27-29, 31, 35, 37-38, 40-41, 48, 51, 56, 59-60,
63-66, 74-76, 79, 89, 91, 93, 95, 104, 108-109, 112, 116, 123, 125-126, 128, 131, 133, 139,
145-146, 148, 151-154,156, 159-160

All other photos courtesy the author

This book is dedicated to my mom. In addition to being the single greatest mom in the world—she's also the real travel bug in our family! She has taught me that "saying yes" to life is the best way to create a lifetime of memories!
I Love You, Mom!

Hey, young readers!

When I was a kid growing up in Wichita, Kansas, the Internet didn't exist (imagine that!), and so my knowledge of this amazing planet was pretty limited. In fact, it wasn't until I started working on *Survivor* that I began to travel to all these crazy, cool places! I now have a map in my house with a pin in every place I have ever visited. There are quite a few pins poked in the map, and yet when I look at all the places I still haven't visited I'm reminded that there is always another adventure to be had!

I hope this book inspires you and reminds you always to seek out your own adventure!

Happy Trails!

Jeff Probst

Note to readers:
See a word in bold? Check out the glossary in the back to find out what it means!

COLDER THAN
ICE

ANTARCTICA
It's no surprise that the coldest place on Earth is on Antarctica.

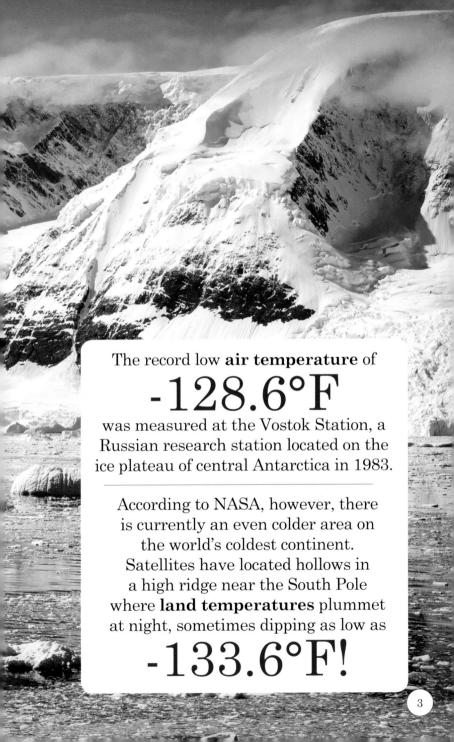

The record low **air temperature** of

-128.6°F

was measured at the Vostok Station, a Russian research station located on the ice plateau of central Antarctica in 1983.

According to NASA, however, there is currently an even colder area on the world's coldest continent. Satellites have located hollows in a high ridge near the South Pole where **land temperatures** plummet at night, sometimes dipping as low as

-133.6°F!

THE WORLD'S TALLEST FOREST

REDWOOD

North America's 470-mile stretch of giant tree groves (along the coast of California, into southern Oregon) is the world's tallest forest. There are about 50 redwood trees taller than 360 feet currently living along the Pacific Coast. That's about the height of a 27-story building!

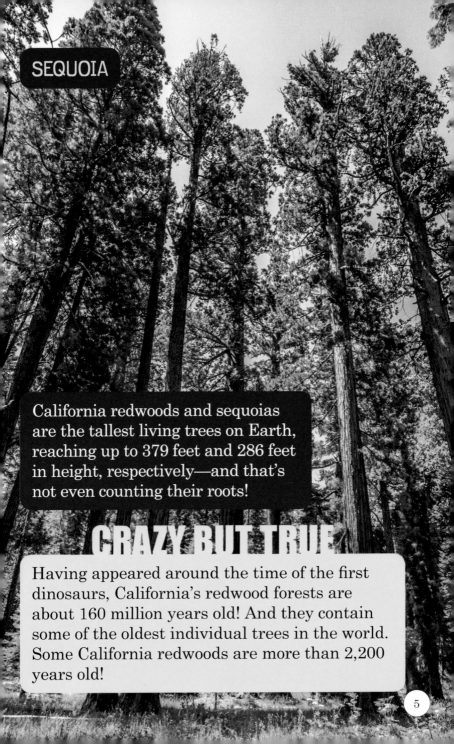

SEQUOIA

California redwoods and sequoias are the tallest living trees on Earth, reaching up to 379 feet and 286 feet in height, respectively—and that's not even counting their roots!

CRAZY BUT TRUE

Having appeared around the time of the first dinosaurs, California's redwood forests are about 160 million years old! And they contain some of the oldest individual trees in the world. Some California redwoods are more than 2,200 years old!

WHAT IS A SEA?

The 1% of surface salt water on Earth not found in the world's oceans can be found in seas and saltwater lakes. Usually bounded by land at the margins of the ocean, seas are subdivisions of oceans and not clearly differentiated from the ocean itself.

There are more than 100 bodies of water known as seas, the largest of which include the Mediterranean Sea, the Caribbean Sea, and the Gulf of Mexico.

CARIBBEAN SEA

CRAZY BUT TRUE

The Sargasso Sea is the only sea on Earth that isn't defined by land boundaries! Instead, it is a region inside the North Atlantic Ocean that is surrounded on all sides by various ocean **currents**. Similar to how the "eye" of a hurricane is relatively calm and still, the Sargasso Sea is clearer and calmer than all of the water around it. It was named after the sargassum seaweed that grows only there, providing food and habitats for an amazing variety of marine species, including turtles, shrimp, crabs, fish, eels, whales, and sharks!

SAND, SAND, & MORE SAND

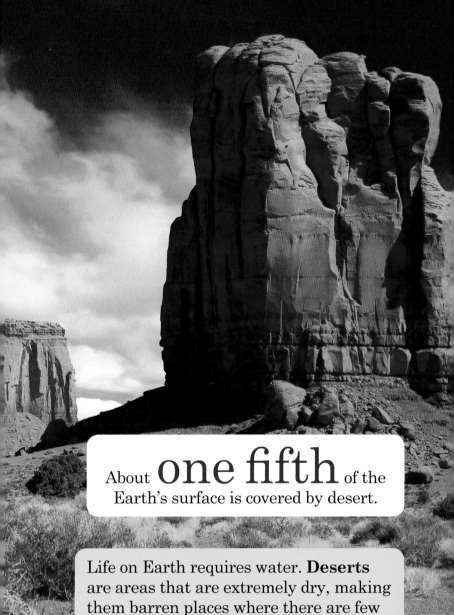

About **one fifth** of the Earth's surface is covered by desert.

Life on Earth requires water. **Deserts** are areas that are extremely dry, making them barren places where there are few living things.

WHITE CLIFFS OF DOVER

Rivaling the majesty of canyon views are vertical sea cliffs found throughout the world.

England's White Cliffs of Dover are white chalk cliffs that face France at the narrowest part of the English Channel. The striking cliffs stand hundreds of feet tall and have served for centuries as a wall against invasion.

CRAZY cliffs

EXTREME CLIFFS

Japan's Cliff of Kurosakitakao stands
1,575 feet
above the ocean's surface.
That's 325 feet taller than the
Empire State Building!

At 2,822 feet, Norway's Hornelen
Mountain is the highest sea cliff
in Europe. At its highest point, it
stands almost 100 feet taller than
the tallest skyscraper in the
world!

About 4,000 feet high,
the top of Canada's Mount Thor is actually
an overhang! It's considered the largest
vertical drop on Earth. And yes, people
actually rock climb there!

UNEXPLORED MARINE LIFE

SALT WATER

A huge portion of all life on Earth lives in salt water, and yet scientists don't know exactly how much. This is because the vast majority of the oceans have yet to be explored.

There are hundreds of species of marine birds, mammals, and reptiles that live in the ocean, as well as countless saltwater invertebrates. There are even

1,500

known species of saltwater fungi!

There are more than

32,700

known species of fish, and more than half of them live in salt water.

The ocean is filled with marine plants, such as seaweed and algae, serving as food, homes, and hiding places for diverse

marine life.

New ocean species are constantly being

discovered!

WETLANDS

Wetlands can be found anywhere there is rain. From the **tundra** to the **tropics**, wetlands can be found in every continent but Antarctica. While many factors go into classifying specific types of wetlands, all share one thing in common: their soil is saturated, if not entirely submerged, beneath water.

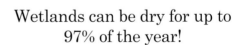

Wetlands can be dry for up to 97% of the year!

Wetland soils, called **hydric soils**, are often gray in color and slippery to the touch, and they can smell like rotting eggs.

Things decompose very slowly in wetland bogs. High soil acidity, cold temperatures, poor water circulation, and a limited oxygen supply all discourage bacteria and other living things from breaking down organic matter.

Which is which? Connect each habitat to its description.

1 Marshes   **3** Bogs

2 Swamps   **4** Fens

A Wetlands with mostly soft-stemmed plants

B Wetlands with a spongy floor covered with sphagnum moss and evergreens

C Wetlands with mostly woody plants, such as cypress trees

D Wetlands with grasses, reeds, and wild-flowers, all growing in a layer of decay

ANSWER: 1=A 2=C 3=B 4=D

CRAZY BUT TRUE

Several ancient human bodies have been discovered naturally mummified by the mud in bogs. One man's body, found in 1950, is believed to be more than 2,000 years old. And he was still wearing his hat!

The plants able to live in parts of the Atacama get their water in unusual ways. Snowmelt from the nearby Andes Mountains makes its way into desert rivers and lakes. But in some areas, marine fog called camanchaca provides the only life support for specially adapted vegetation.

CRAZY BUT TRUE

Some people still call the driest place on Earth home! Villagers who live in areas blessed with fog have made camanchaca "nets" out of screens. They use them to collect drinking water right out of the air!

THE DRIEST PLACE ON EARTH

ATACAMA DESERT

In parts of the Atacama Desert, a **coastal desert** in western South America, years pass without a single drop of rain! In fact, researchers believe one region in the center of 41,000 square miles of **desert** didn't see rainfall for 400 years! Not a single animal calls that part of the Atacama Desert home. And neither do any plants—not even a single cactus!

17

WORLD-FAMOUS VOLCANOES

MOUNT YASUR
For over 800 years, Mount Yasur, in Vanuatu (east of Australia), has been free of vegetation because of frequent lava flows. It erupts several times an hour!

KILAUEA

Kilauea, the most famous of Hawaii's volcanoes, has been continuously erupting for more than 30 years! It feeds two separate **lava** lakes with fresh lava!

19

MOUNT ETNA

Two Mediterranean volcanoes named Mount Etna and Mount Stromboli near Sicily, Italy, have also been in "almost continuous eruption" since antiquity. That means they've been erupting for more than 2,000 years!

MOUNT STROMBOLI

NEIGHBORHOOD WATCH!

The International Association of Volcanology and Chemistry of the Earth's Interior (IAVCEI) has identified 17 "Decade Volcanoes." Located on every continent but Antarctica, these volcanoes are near populated areas and have a history of enormous, destructive eruptions! The two located within the United States are Mauna Loa in Hawaii and Mount Rainier in Washington State.

WANT SOME FRESHWATER?

Lakes contain about 90% of all the non-ocean surface water found on Earth!

Earth's Puzzle Pieces

GREENLAND

Greenland is the world's largest island, and it was once a part of North America. New Guinea was once a part of Australia. Borneo was once a part of the mainland of Asia. Madagascar once touched parts of Africa and India. And so on.

Islands that aren't built from cooled **lava** are most often **continental islands**, meaning they are made of land that split off from larger continents.

There are also artificial, or man-made, islands. Though usually quite small, some of the world's artificial islands are larger than natural islands! The island of Flevopolder in Flevoland, Netherlands, is 370 square miles! It is more than 23 times larger than any other artificial island.

CRAZY BUT TRUE

Geologists believe that all of these puzzle pieces once fit together to form a single landmass, called Pangaea! In fact, if you look at a map, you can see how North and South America fit cleanly together with Africa and Europe.

GREAT LAKES

The Great Lakes formed 10,000 years ago, at the end of the Ice Age. Huge sheets of ice cut deep into the ground and then, melting, filled the lake **basin** with water.

Want a trick to remembering all of the Great Lakes? The first letters of their names spell the word *homes*! It helps to think of all the fish and other animals that live in them.

The Great Lakes collectively contain 21% of the world's surface freshwater and more than half of the world's liquid freshwater by **volume**.

LAKE SUPERIOR

TRUE OR FALSE?
The Great Lakes
contain enough
water to cover all
of North and South
America.

CHALLENGE
YOURSELF!

ANSWER: True! Lake Superior *alone*
contains enough water to cover all of
North and South America with a foot of water!

27

LAKE SUPERIOR

GREAT LAKES
The largest group of fresh-water lakes on Earth can be found in North America, bordered by both the United States and Canada. These Great Lakes include Lake Huron, Lake Ontario, Lake Michigan, Lake Erie, and Lake Superior.

LAKE MICHIGAN

LAKE HURON

LAKE ONTARIO

LAKE ERIE

DON'T MAKE ME GO!

Two towns in northeastern Siberia are tied for the coldest permanently inhabited places on Earth! Oymyakon and Verkhoyansk, both in Russia, each noted record lows of -90°F, the lowest recorded temperature in the **Northern Hemisphere**.

Several hundred people call Oymyakon home. And twice as many live in Verkhoyansk, which was established as a place to send political exiles. In both places, the ground is permanently frozen, and average monthly temperatures remain below freezing for 7 months of the year!

CRAZY BUT TRUE

In Oymyakon, schools stay open through weather as cold as -60°F! Never mind your snowshoes. You might need to pack a survival kit!

OYMYAKON

VERKHOYANSK

LET IT SNOW!

The island of Japan surprisingly includes the snowiest place on Earth! Bombarded with Siberian winter winds, Sukayu Onsen, Japan, has an average yearly snowfall of 58 feet, with some years bringing 70 or 80 feet of snow! It also holds the record for the highest depth of snow collected on the ground. Imagine white canyons of snow, rising 10 to 15 feet above your head! Luckily, the region is also home to hot springs. The residents of Sukayu Onsen are gonna need them!

THE MIGHTY NILE

NILE RIVER

Africa's Nile River is the longest—but not the largest!—river in the world. Stretching more than 4,258 miles, the Nile flows through Egypt, Sudan, Kenya, Eritrea, Democratic Republic of the Congo, Burundi, Uganda, Tanzania, Rwanda, and Ethiopia.

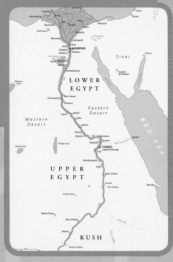

The Nile River is so long and treacherous that navigating its full length is a historic occasion! In fact, it wasn't until 2004 that a group first achieved the feat. It took an international team of whitewater rafters 4 months and 2 weeks to complete the expedition. They even made an IMAX movie about the explorers' epic journey!

THE RING OF FIRE!

There are around 1,500 active volcanoes in the world. About 90% of them are located in what has come to be known as the Ring of Fire. Sometimes called the circum-Pacific belt—because it forms a horseshoe around the Pacific Ocean—the Ring of Fire is also where 17% of the world's largest earthquakes occur.

SEA ICE SURROUNDS
THE VOLCANIC ISLAND
OF SHIKOTAN

Though the surface of the Earth appears stable, beneath a relatively thin **crust** lies a churning core of **magma**, molten rock heated to a liquid. The ground as we know it is actually a series of interlocking plates, like puzzle pieces. Volcanoes form anywhere magma escapes between them.

PANTANAL

The largest **wetland** of any kind, the Pantanal extends an estimated 75,000 square miles from western Brazil into Bolivia and Paraguay. Millions of capybaras call the Pantanal home, as does one of the largest populations of jaguars on Earth!

ISIMANGALISO WETLAND PARK

iSimangaliso Wetland Park on the east coast of KwaZulu-Natal, South Africa, is the country's third-largest protected area and contains most of its remaining wetlands. The name means "miracle and wonder" in Zulu. More than 1,200 Nile crocodiles and 800 hippopotamuses live there, along with 526 bird species.

EVERGLADES

The Everglades of Florida in the
United States extends from Lake
Okeechobee to the Florida Bay and
is the largest subtropical wetland
ecosystem in North America. It is
the only place on Earth where the
American alligator and American
crocodile share a natural habitat.

37

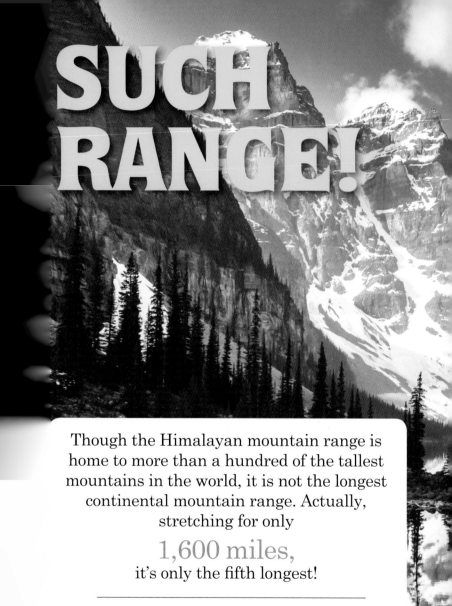

SUCH RANGE!

Though the Himalayan mountain range is home to more than a hundred of the tallest mountains in the world, it is not the longest continental mountain range. Actually, stretching for only

1,600 miles,
it's only the fifth longest!

Stretching for 3,000 miles, the Rocky Mountains of North America form the third-longest continental mountain range.

ROCKY
MOUNTAINS

HUANG HO RIVER

Known popularly as the Yellow River, the Huang Ho is considered the deadliest river in the world. Thousands of people die annually due to the river's flooding, with an estimated 5 million deaths reported in the past hundred years. For this reason, it's also nicknamed China's Sorrow.

CONGO RIVER

The second-largest river in the world by **volume** of water, the Congo River in Africa reaches depths of 720 feet, making it the deepest river in the world! It is also the most powerful river in Africa.

PUERTO PRINCESA

The Puerto Princesa River in Palawan, Philippines, is subterranean, meaning that it flows underground! In fact, it is considered the world's longest navigable subterranean river. In 2011, it was named one of the New 7 Wonders of Nature, the only river in the world to receive the honor.

ROE RIVER

The Roe River in Great Falls, Montana, was named the world's shortest river by the *Guinness World Records*. The Roe River flows for only 200 feet, between Giant Springs and the Missouri River.

41

VICTORIA FALLS

Though Victoria Falls in Zimbabwe is neither the highest nor the widest waterfall in the world, its combined height and width create the largest sheet of falling water on Earth! Part of the Zambezi River, Victoria Falls is 354 feet tall, roughly twice the height of North America's Niagara Falls!

ARIZONA'S HORSESHOE BEND

The 17-million-year-old Colorado River cuts through 7 U.S. states and 2 Mexican states. It is the river responsible for carving Arizona's 277-mile-long Grand Canyon 4,000 to 6,000 feet deep through layers of rock. It is also responsible for Horseshoe Bend, just outside of Page, Arizona.

Most canyons form through **erosion**. River water cuts through the ground, washing sediment downstream. Over time, a river can cut a deep channel into the ground—even through rock!

ECHIDNA CHASM

Echidna Chasm in Australia is a slot canyon, meaning it is very narrow. It's only 6 feet wide in places, yet hundreds of feet deep. In fact, its walls are almost 3 times taller than San Francisco's Golden Gate Bridge!

Some canyons are formed when underground river caves

collapse!

COLCA CANYON

The Colca Canyon in Peru is twice as deep as the Grand Canyon!

VERDON GORGE

Perhaps Europe's most scenic canyon, the Verdon Gorge in France has turquoise-blue water and light-colored limestone walls.

COPPER CANYON

Copper Canyon in Mexico is a system of 6 canyons formed by 6 different rivers.

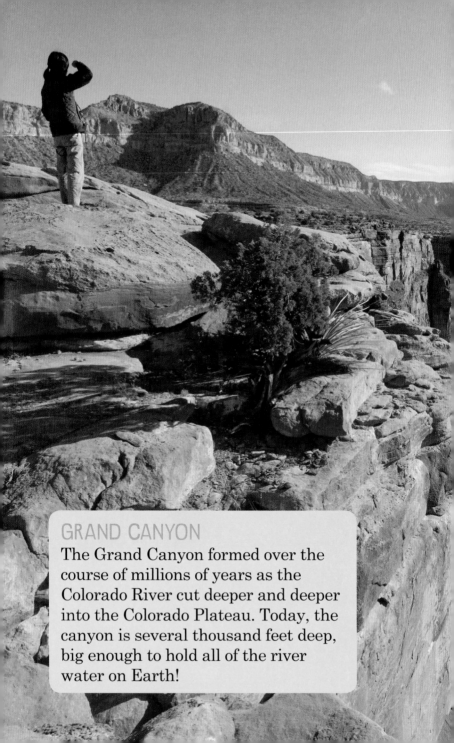

GRAND CANYON

The Grand Canyon formed over the course of millions of years as the Colorado River cut deeper and deeper into the Colorado Plateau. Today, the canyon is several thousand feet deep, big enough to hold all of the river water on Earth!

ACTIVE VOLCANOES!

CHALLENGE YOURSELF!

Ancient cultures believed volcanoes were the result of which of the following?

A Punishments for human actions

B Monsters

C Giants living inside the mountains

D All of the above!

ANSWER: D!
Ancient people made up all sorts of fantastic legends to explain what volcanoes were and why they erupted. Today, scientists know more about volcanoes than they ever have before.

I actually stood on the edge of one of the most active of the volcanoes in the Ring of Fire: Mount Yasur in Vanuatu! We were shooting the opening sequence for *Survivor: Vanuatu.* That baby was blowing like crazy, with lava spraying everywhere! It was one of the coolest and probably craziest things I've ever experienced.

A THOUSAND MILES OF CORAL!

GREAT BARRIER REEF

The Great Barrier Reef off the coast of Australia is the largest and most famous coral reef on Earth. It is more than 1,400 miles long, and it is made up of more than 2,900 individual reefs and 900 islands. More than 1,500 fish species live there, alongside 7 species of sea snakes and 30 species of whales, dolphins, and porpoises, as well as a great many other plants and animals.

CRAZY BUT TRUE

There are such things as artificial reefs, where sponges and corals grow onto sunken ships, oil rigs, M60 army tanks—even discarded subway cars! For decades, humans have been intentionally sinking these massive metal objects in the hopes of creating hurricane-proof habitats for coral to grow. It's even the job of some people to dive down to check on how things are doing!

ICICLES OF ROCK

The words *stalactite* and *stalag-mite* look and sound similar. It's easy to confuse the two! Want a way to remember which points up and which points down? One of the words has a *c* in it, as in *ceiling,* while the other has a *g,* as in *ground*.

STALAGMITES

If you've ever been in a cave, you might have noticed strange-looking rock formations. Some formations build upward from the cave floor. These conical deposits are called **stalagmites**. They form when water dripping from the stalactites causes minerals to accumulate on the ground.

STALACTITES

Stalactites look like icicles made of rock! And they form in much the same way! When water drips into the cave through the limestone, it carries various minerals in with it. Over time, these minerals build up and harden—much like water hardens into an icicle as it drips and freezes.

Many more strange rock formations can be found in caves. Flowstones, which are created much like stalactites, can form sheetlike translucent "curtains"! Massive crystals, cylindrical "soda straws," and even 20-foot gypsum "chandeliers" appear in the world's underground hiding places!

BIG RIVER!

VENEZUELA

GUYANA

SURI FRENCH

BIA

AMAZON RIVER
The Amazon River in South America
is the largest river in the world.

Amazon

Manaus

Rio Branco

BR

S

SILIA

AMAZON RIVER

B

o

ban

CHILE

o

Porto Ale

ARGENTINA

URUGUAY

Though the Nile is officially the longest river, the Amazon contains more water. In fact, more water flows through the Amazon than through the 7 next-largest rivers combined, totaling 16% of all the world's river water!

It might also be the world's scariest river! Some of the world's most treacherous animals call the Amazon River home, including piranhas, vampire fish, candirú, leeches, electric eels, bull sharks, and anacondas, the largest snakes in the world.

We shot the sixth season of *Survivor* in the Amazon. Every night after tribal council we would take a small fishing boat back to our room. We would shine our flashlights along the banks of the Rio Negro and see the eyes of black caimans (a type of crocodile)! It was exciting, eerie, and a little bit scary!

CORAL CLOSE-UP

Coral grows very, very slowly. Most coral grows as little as $\frac{1}{4}$ of an inch per year! Therefore, coral reefs grow very slowly, too. Some coral reefs today started growing 50 million years ago or more! Most, however, are somewhere between 5,000 and 10,000 years old.

Countless Colors of Coral!

SMALLER THAN THEY LOOK

A living coral, called a polyp, is only $\frac{1}{10}$ of an inch long! Each head of coral is actually a vast colony of identical coral polyps growing together in one place and sharing resources.

Though most coral does secrete toxic chemicals, several fish and other animals eat coral, including parrot fish, butterfly fish, angelfish, sea slugs, snails, worms, and starfish.

nurseries
of the
SEA

CRAZY BUT TRUE

The Chesapeake Bay, the largest estuary in the United States, is responsible for more seafood per mile than any other place on Earth! Anchovies, trout, bluefish, flounder, oysters, blue crabs, and various bass and catfish all call the Chesapeake Bay home. All told, more than 250 species of fish and 300 species of migratory birds spend at least a portion of their life cycles in the 64,000-square-mile watershed.

ESTUARIES

Estuaries are partially enclosed bodies of water where freshwater mixes with salt water. They often form where rivers meet the ocean.

Estuaries are great nesting grounds because they are close to oceans and offer a protected environment and abundant food sources. Thousands of birds and fish begin their life in estuaries!

Estuaries also serve as massive filters, keeping excessive pollution and sediment from dumping into the sea from freshwater rivers. They act as a buffer zone between the turbulent ocean and the shore, protecting land habitats from flooding and from storm surges.

THIS DESERT IS DEPRESSED

TAKLIMAKAN DESERT

The largest, hottest, and driest **desert** in China—the Taklimakan Desert—is also one of the world's largest shifting-sand deserts. Located in the depression of the Tarim **basin** and surrounded by mountains, the desert has been collecting sand since the Taklimakan's formation. Considered hazardous to cross, 85% of the region is made up of shifting sand dunes!

CRAZY BUT TRUE

If you look at a **topographic map** of a shifting-sand desert, it appears flat, even though it isn't! Imagine mountains of sand that change their location slowly as the wind blows, some of which grow to be 1,000 feet high or more. Mapmakers, called cartographers, don't include these dunes—not because they aren't there, but because they want their maps to be accurate and they can't predict where dunes will pile up next.

MONUMENT VALLEY

MONUMENT VALLEY

Located on the border between Arizona and Utah, Monument Valley is an iconic American West landscape and one of the most photographed scenes on Earth. Red sandstone buttes tower amid vast desert plains.

Not an actual valley, Monument Valley is a flat expanse of land within the Great Basin Desert. It actually has an elevation of about

5,000 feet.

At one point, the elevation of the area was even higher. Over time, the sandstone in the area eroded, leaving behind the buttes and mesas still visible today.

CRAZY BUT TRUE

More than 1 billion years old, the Blue Ridge Mountains (part of North America's Appalachian Mountain range) are the oldest mountains in the United States. They're at least 12 ½ times older than the Rocky Mountains! They're also more than twice as old as the Himalayas. And yet, they're not the oldest mountains in the world. Not even close! South Africa's Barberton Greenstone Mountain belt is three times older, with an estimated age of 3.6 billion years.

OLD MOUNTAINS

BLUE RIDGE MOUNTAINS

Which of the following is the longest continental mountain range?

A The Rocky Mountains

B The Andes Mountains

C The Swiss Alps

ANSWER: **B!**
The Andes, a chain of mountains in South America, is the longest. It stretches for 4,350 miles down the west coast of the continent. North to south, the Andes consist of hundreds of summits in the countries of Venezuela, Colombia, Ecuador, Peru, Bolivia, Chile, and Argentina.

COLD DESERTS?! ARE YOU AN OXYMORON?

ANTARCTICA

Not all **deserts** are hot! Regions are classified as deserts when they have extremely low amounts of rain or other **precipitation**. Some of the world's most extreme deserts are actually freezing! There, the air is too cold to hold much moisture.

There are large **cold deserts** in Central Asia, as well as in North and South America.

CRAZY BUT TRUE

Did you know Antarctica is a desert? In fact, it's the largest desert on Earth! It is considered a **polar desert**, because it is located at one of the Earth's two poles. Since it's made up of about 98% ice and 2% barren rock, you can bet it's cold! The South Pole itself has never had a recorded temperature above 9.9°F, and it receives less than 4 inches of precipitation a year. That's cold *and* dry.

AND THE GREEN GRASS GREW ALL AROUND

Also called prairies, pampas, steppes, and savannas, **grasslands** are **biomes** made mostly of grasses. They are found on every continent, except for Antarctica.

Tropical grasslands, such as savannas, can be found near the **Equator**. The world's most diverse collection of hoofed mammals is found on the savannas of Africa, considered the largest expanse of grasslands in the world! Other tropical grassland animals include buffaloes, kangaroos, mice, moles, termites, worms, and elephants.

Temperate grasslands are found in milder climates, including the pampas of South America, the steppes of Eurasia, and the plains of North America. North American grassland animals include bison, prairie dogs, coyotes, foxes, meadowlarks, quails, and hawks.

SERENGETI GRASSLANDS

Only 2% of North America's original grassland remains. Most of the prairie land of the United States has been converted into farmland. Thanks to the naturally rich soils of grasslands, the midwestern United States is one of the richest agricultural regions on Earth!

ONE CRAZY CAVE!

REED FLUTE CAVE, CHINA

The Reed Flute Cave in China gets its name from the special reeds that grow outside and that can be made into flutes. Inside, the 180-million-year-old cave is filled with weird and wonderful rock formations and colorful artificial lighting. There are also more than 70 written inscriptions, some of which date back as far as the Tang Dynasty in 792 AD!

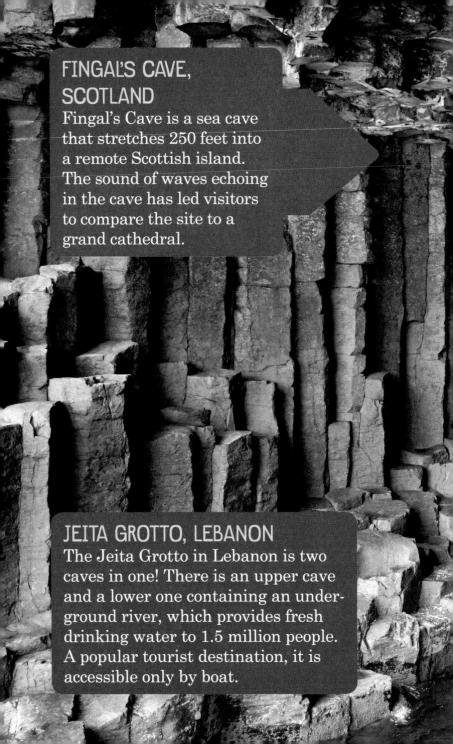

FINGAL'S CAVE, SCOTLAND

Fingal's Cave is a sea cave that stretches 250 feet into a remote Scottish island. The sound of waves echoing in the cave has led visitors to compare the site to a grand cathedral.

JEITA GROTTO, LEBANON

The Jeita Grotto in Lebanon is two caves in one! There is an upper cave and a lower one containing an underground river, which provides fresh drinking water to 1.5 million people. A popular tourist destination, it is accessible only by boat.

GIANT CRYSTAL CAVE, MEXICO

Some of the largest natural crystals ever found were discovered in Chihuahua, Mexico, where, nearly 1,000 feet below the Earth's surface, **lava**-heated, mineral-rich water formed Giant Crystal Cave.

EISRIESENWELT, AUSTRIA

The largest known ice cave in the world, Austria's Eisriesenwelt is a cave nestled in the Alps mountain chain. The name means "World of the Ice Giants" in German. Before it was explored in the 1800s, locals believed it was an entrance to the underworld.

The Windiest Places on Earth

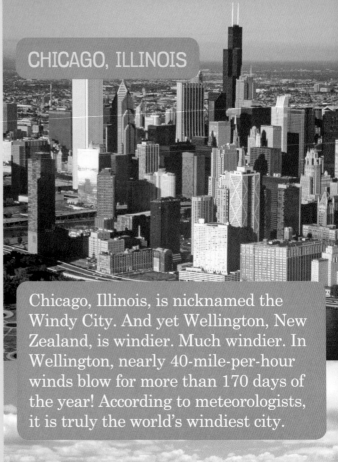

CHICAGO, ILLINOIS

Chicago, Illinois, is nicknamed the Windy City. And yet Wellington, New Zealand, is windier. Much windier. In Wellington, nearly 40-mile-per-hour winds blow for more than 170 days of the year! According to meteorologists, it is truly the world's windiest city.

WELLINGTON, NEW ZEALAND

The two windiest places on Earth aren't cities at all! To establish a city in either, buildings would have to withstand regular hurricane-strength winds! One is near the North Pole, and the other is near the South Pole.

Up in Cape Farewell, Greenland, gale-force winds called the Greenland tip jet blow through at nearly 45 miles per hour, ripping the tops off waves!

Down in Antarctica, meteorologists have described an "almost continuous blizzard," where explorers are unable to see more than an arm's length in front of them. Winds whipping around the cliff of Cape Denison reach an average annual speed of nearly 50 miles per hour! And one explorer, named Douglas Mawson, claimed to have witnessed gusts approaching 200 miles per hour!

OUR BLUE PLANET

Almost three quarters of the Earth's surface is covered in salt water, the vast majority of which is divided by 7 land continents into 7 interconnected ocean territories: the North and South Pacific Oceans, the North and South Atlantic Oceans, the Indian Ocean, the Southern Ocean, and the Arctic Ocean.

According to oceanographers, only about 5% of our oceans have been explored! In fact, we have better maps of the surface of Mars than we do of our own ocean floor! Several hundred people have been sent into space, and yet only 3 people have been to the deepest part of the ocean. There is so much left to discover!

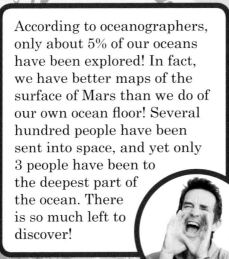

TRUE OR FALSE?
The world's oceans contain 97% of all of Earth's water.

CHALLENGE YOURSELF!

ANSWER: True! Life on Earth began in the world's oceans, and without them human life on land would be impossible! About half of the world's population lives along the oceans' coastlines, and oceans produce more than half of the oxygen in our atmosphere!

One out of every 4 ingredients in our medicine was first discovered in rain-forest plants. The U.S. National Cancer Institute identified 3,000 plants that are active against cancer cells, and the vast majority of them were first found in the **rain forest**. Imagine all of the medicines that are still out there waiting to be discovered!

THE EARTH PROVIDES

More than 80% of the food we eat first grew in **tropical** rain forests, before being farmed elsewhere. This includes many popular foods around the world: avocados, oranges, lemons, bananas, pineapples, tomatoes, potatoes, coffee, sugarcane, cinnamon, pepper, many kinds of nuts, and much, much more.

Together, tropical and temperate rain forests are responsible for 28% of the world's oxygen turnover! Imagine one out of every four of your breaths! That's a lot of air, isn't it?

About 2,000 trees per minute are cut down in the rain forests; that's nearly 34 trees every single second. Think about that. And they don't grow back nearly as fast. Most of those trees took hundreds and sometimes thousands of years to grow.

If you were to count up every kind of fruit eaten in the United States, the number would account for only a fraction of the 3,000 known fruits that grow wild in the rain forests of the world.

RAIN, RAIN, GO AWAY!

MOUNT WAIALEALE

The wettest place on Earth is Mawsynram, a village in Meghalaya, India, which has an annual rainfall of 467.4 inches. According to the *Guinness World Records,* Mawsynram received 1,000 inches of rain in 1985.

Mount Waialeale in Hawaii is a close second, averaging more than 450 inches of rain each year. There, it rains between 330 and 360 days a year! Imagine a year in which it rained for all but 5 days. It would be very hard to keep dry.

GALÁPAGOS ISLANDS

The Galápagos Islands are a cluster of islands 575 miles off the west coast of Ecuador, in South America. During a visit to the islands in the 1830s, a scientist named Charles Darwin made observations about animals living in isolation that led to his theory of natural selection. Darwin's theories about the development of animal species are central to our modern understanding of the theory of evolution.

MADAGASCAR

Madagascar, off the coast of East Africa, is home to 250,000 species of wildlife. Due to the relative isolation of the island, 70% of the island's species are unique to Madagascar.

SOCOTRA ISLAND, YEMEN

Located 150 miles east of the Horn of Africa and 240 miles south of the Arabian Peninsula, Yemen's Socotra Island has been described as looking like an alien planet! This is likely because it is the most isolated **continental island**. Some 700 species found on Socotra live nowhere else on Earth, including the famous dragon tree.

SITING ON A VOLCANO

YELLOWSTONE NATIONAL PARK

Yellowstone National Park in Wyoming covers more than 2 million acres and is considered one of the most amazing natural attractions on Earth. It was the world's first designated national park, and contains a 20-mile-long canyon, sweeping **grasslands**, and 17 rivers.

The park also sits on one of the largest volcanoes in the world. Scientists estimate that the lake of **magma** below Yellowstone is three times larger than Lake Michigan!

The volcanic activity of the area is also responsible for some of Yellowstone's most amazing sights, including **geysers**, colorful hot springs, steaming craters called **fumaroles**, and bubbling mud pots. All told, there are an estimated 10,000 thermal features in the area.

MOTHER NATURE'S CLOCK?

Known as the most predictable geographical feature on Earth, Old Faithful is no ordinary geyser. It erupts a blast of water every 91 minutes— almost exactly!

HIDDEN ROOMS

Also called caverns, caves form in a variety of ways. But most caves are "solutional caves," formed when water-soluble rock erodes.

There are more limestone caves in the world than any other kind!

The recreational exploration of caves is called **spelunking**, while the study of caves is known as **speleology**.

STRANGE SEAS

CASPIAN SEA

Sometimes called the world's largest lake, the Caspian Sea is considered an **inland sea**, and the largest enclosed inland body of water on Earth. It is also among the saltiest!

BLACK SEA

Another inland sea, the Black Sea, connects Europe and Asia Minor. It is unique for the way its deep and shallow waters do not mix! As a result, 90% of its deep water contains very little oxygen, without which micro-organisms have a hard time decomposing things. According to marine archaeologists, a great many ancient wooden shipwrecks lie perfectly preserved at the bed of this sea!

DEAD SEA

The Dead Sea between Jordan, Palestine, and Israel is among the saltiest, too. In fact, some people call it the Salt Sea! Located at Earth's lowest elevation point on land, the Dead Sea is almost 10 times saltier than the ocean! It's so salty that fish and seaweed can't survive in it—hence the name.

CRAZY BUT TRUE

The Dead Sea is possibly the worst place to fish, but it's a pretty great place to swim! In fact, when people swim in the Dead Sea, they float a lot more easily than they do in regular water. Here's why: the Dead Sea has a lot of salt in it, and salt water is heavy (way heavier than regular water). In order for you to float, the water has to weigh as much if not more than you. The salt water in the Dead Sea does, and that's why it's so easy to float there!

THE WORLD'S LARGEST FORESTS

BOREAL FORESTS

Twice the size of the Amazonian **rain forest**, the vast **boreal forests** of Russia stretch for more than 3 million square miles, from Karelia near Finland to the Kamchatka Peninsula far to the east. Also called taiga, these forests cover about half of Russia's entire landmass! They contain 50% of the world's coniferous wood!

An amazing 93% of Canada's forests are publicly owned!

CHALLENGE YOURSELF!

Russia's boreal forests also house countless species of animals, including which of the following?

A Siberian tigers

B Snow monkeys

C Asian elephants

ANSWER: A!
About 10% of all wild tigers are found in these vast forests, as well as snow leopards and the world's biggest owl.

NOT A
TEA KETTLE

The majority of lakes in the world are "kettle lakes" produced by glacial activity long ago. At the end of the Ice Age, melting glaciers left their marks on the land below, forming impressions called kettles that remain filled with water to this day.

THESE PLACES ROCK!

STONE FOREST, CHINA
The Stone Forest in Yunnan Province, China, isn't really a forest at all. The 270-million-year-old formations are actually made of limestone and not **petrified wood**.

DEVILS TOWER, WYOMING
The first National Monument in the United States, Devils Tower is a 5,114-foot tower of **igneous rock**, having formed from cooled **lava**. Exactly how it was formed remains a mystery.

PETRA, JORDAN

The ancient city of Petra, Jordan, was partially carved out of rock. In fact, the word *petra* means rock! Surrounded by mountains and primarily accessible through long canyon passages, Petra was essentially a fortress city, carved into desert rock.

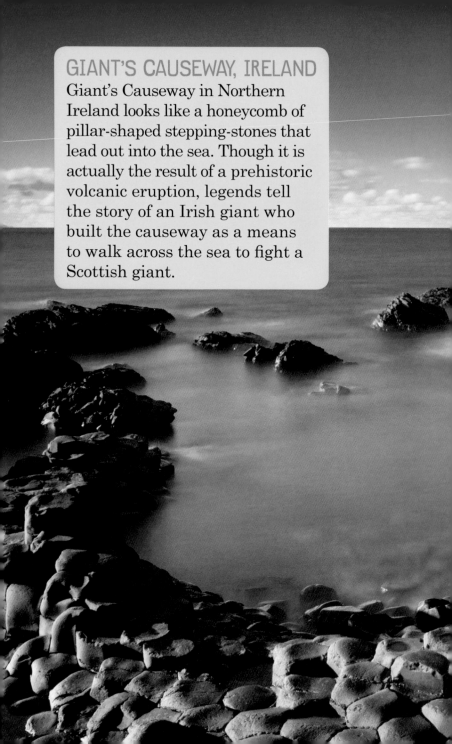

GIANT'S CAUSEWAY, IRELAND

Giant's Causeway in Northern Ireland looks like a honeycomb of pillar-shaped stepping-stones that lead out into the sea. Though it is actually the result of a prehistoric volcanic eruption, legends tell the story of an Irish giant who built the causeway as a means to walk across the sea to fight a Scottish giant.

CRAZY BUT TRUE

There are identical columns across the sea in Scotland! Though the matching pillars are the result of the same **lava** flow, it's no wonder folks came up with the legend to explain the strange stones.

THE TWELVE APOSTLES, AUSTRALIA

Also known as the Gibson Steps, the Twelve Apostles is a collection of limestone stacks off the southern coast of Australia. They formed by **erosion**, as seawater dug caves and archways into the limestone, gradually eating away at the rock until nothing was left but the roughly 150-foot-tall rocks.

CRAZY BUT TRUE

Despite the name, geologists believe there were only ever 9 stacks, instead of 12. In 2005, continuing wave erosion caused one of the large rocks to collapse into the water. Today, only 8 of them remain.

"COTTON CASTLE," TURKEY

Southwestern Turkey is home to Pamukkale, which means "Cotton Castle" in Turkish. The bone-white limestone terraces found at Pamukkale were formed by 17 hot-water springs, which have deposited hardening minerals for at least 2,000 years.

PETRIFIED WOOD

Much like dinosaur bones, plants can become fossilized, meaning that their organic tissues are slowly replaced by minerals. In some cases, the trees of ancient forests have turned into **petrified wood**! The resulting **fossil** preserves the original structure of the wood, like a 3-D model made of colorful stone.

The world's largest petrified forest is in Greece, on the island of Lesbos. Petrified wood covers

93 square miles

of the island, including large upright tree trunks with their root systems intact!

PETRIFIED FOREST

When many trees in the same area become petrified, they call it a petrified forest. Petrified forests can be found all over the world, including a dozen U.S. states.

Among the most celebrated petrified forests in the United States, the Petrified Forest National Park in Arizona is known for fossils more than 10 times older than those in Greece. Some of the petrified logs found there are about 225 million years old!

TIDAL ISLANDS

Islands connected by a causeway or strip of land accessible only at low **tide** are called tidal islands. More than half a mile off the northwest coast of France, Mont Saint-Michel is perhaps the most famous tidal island community in the world.

Access to the island has changed in recent years. In 2014, a new bridge above the existing causeway was opened to the public, allowing for the removal of a 125-year-old causeway that was once the only connection between the island and the French mainland.

One of France's top five tourist attractions, Mont Saint-Michel has a permanent population of only 43 people, half of them monks!

MONT SAINT-MICHEL

It is estimated that 70% of the world's coral reefs will disappear in the next 40 years, because of pollution, coral mining, destructive fishing practices, and ocean warming. This is terrible not only for the animals that live there; coral reefs also serve coastal land regions, protecting humans and land animals from powerful waves and storms.

CRAZY BUT TRUE

Corals look like plants, because they often have branches and stay fixed in one place. But in truth, they're very small animals! And what look like rocks below them are actually the limestone skeletons of previous generations of coral.

CORAL REEF
One quarter of all ocean life can be found in coral reefs that cover less than 0.1% of the ocean floor. That's like a Band-Aid at the bottom of an Olympic-size pool!

reindeer country!

TUNDRA

The coldest **biomes** on Earth, **tundras** are found in the far north and on the tops of mountains, where part of the ground remains permanently frozen. Grasses grow on tundra, as do small shrubs, sedges, mosses, and lichens. Rare scattered trees can grow there, too, but only those adapted to the harsh climate.

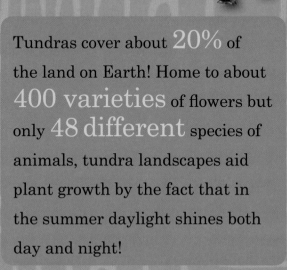

Tundras cover about 20% of the land on Earth! Home to about 400 varieties of flowers but only 48 different species of animals, tundra landscapes aid plant growth by the fact that in the summer daylight shines both day and night!

TRUE OR FALSE?
Humans can't live
in harsh tundra
landscapes.

CHALLENGE YOURSELF!

ANSWER: **False!** The Inuit
people have lived there for
hundreds of years!

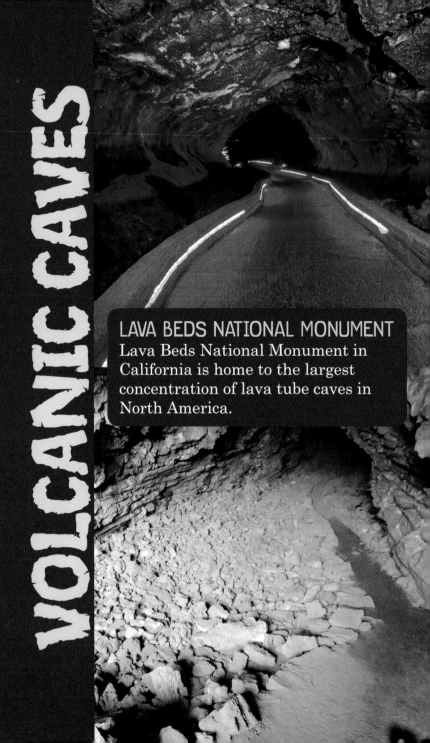

VOLCANIC CAVES

LAVA BEDS NATIONAL MONUMENT

Lava Beds National Monument in California is home to the largest concentration of lava tube caves in North America.

Most caves form through erosion, but others are forged by which volcanic activity?

A Volcanic smoke pushes pockets of air into rock

B Explosions partially bury canyons with debris

C Lava tubes leave hollows in the ground

ANSWER: **C!**
Lava tubes form when hot **lava** pours out of an underground volcano! As the molten lava tunnels through the ground, the edges of the flow cool and harden, forming a hollow tube.

The world's largest singular lava tube is in Kazumura Cave, in Hawaii. The greatest linear stretch of Kazumura is 40.7 miles long, making it the longest of any cave known to man! That's roughly the length of the city of Boston's underground subway system!

THE GRANDER CANYON!

YARLUNG TSANGPO RIVER

Nestled high in the Himalayan mountain range, the Yarlung Tsangpo River in Tibet is the highest river in the world. Tsangpo Grand Canyon, carved by Tibet's "Mother River," is both longer and deeper than North America's Grand Canyon. In fact, Tsangpo Canyon reaches a depth of 19,714 feet, more than 3 times deeper!

In 2002, an international team of 7 kayakers became the first to navigate the initial descent of the legendary upper Tsangpo gorge successfully. To this day, no one has successfully run the rapids of the lower gorge!

Due to cold temperatures, 70- to 100-foot waterfalls, and other extreme conditions, the Yarlung Tsangpo River has been called the Everest of Rivers and is a destination for the world's most daring whitewater explorers. Several expert kayakers have died tragically while attempting to paddle through the Yarlung Tsangpo Canyon gorge, which Buddhists consider to be sacred. Yet others continue to try to run the "unrunnable rapids"!

mysteries of the Amazon

AMAZON RIVER SYSTEM

Not all of the animals found in the Amazon River have been identified. The Amazon River system is home to countless animals, including 1,500 known fish species and 8,000 species of insects—with many others yet to be discovered. Imagine what monstrous animals might still be hiding in the Amazon's vast waters!

CRAZY BUT TRUE

Despite these dangers, someone actually swam the length of the Amazon! A Slovenian long-distance swimmer named Martin Strel swam the river in 2007. It took him 66 days to complete the record-breaking 3,273-mile journey. Strel also holds records for successfully swimming other rivers, including the Danube, the Mississippi, and the Yangtze.

Guess how many bridges cross the Amazon River.

CHALLENGE YOURSELF!

None! Even though the Amazon River is the second longest in the world, there are no bridges that cross it! Though one comes close. The colossal Rio Negro Bridge opened in 2011, spanning 11,795 feet across the Rio Negro, which empties into the Amazon.

SUPER-SCARY LAKES

BOILING LAKE

No Swimming! Boiling Lake, situated in a national park on the Caribbean island of Dominica, has water so hot that it actively boils at the center! Scientists believe the lake is actually a flooded **fumarole**, a hole in the Earth's **crust**, with molten **lava** hidden below the churning water.

LAKE NYOS

Three volcanic lakes in central Africa are the only known "exploding lakes" on Earth. Carbon dioxide seeps up from **magma** below the lake bed, charging the water and turning it into carbonic acid. In 1986, one such lake near Cameroon released a cloud of carbon dioxide so large that it killed nearly 2,000 people and upward of 4,500 livestock!

JELLYFISH LAKE

Resting in the western Pacific Ocean, Palau's Jellyfish Lake is home to millions of—you guessed it—jellyfish! Unlike other species, however, the golden jellyfish that reside in the isolated lake have such a light sting that they don't hurt humans. In fact, scary as they might appear, they're safe to swim with!

SAHARAN SAND DUNES

The largest nonpolar **desert** in the world is the Sahara Desert in North Africa. It is about the size of the entire United States! The countries of Egypt, Libya, Chad, Algeria, Morocco, Niger, Sudan, and Tunisia are all covered by the desert.

KALAHARI DESERT

Like most deserts, the Kalahari Desert in Southern Africa has huge temperature swings. In the hot sun, the temperature rises to a sweltering 104°F. But at night, the temperature drops dramatically to 0°F or lower!

LAVA &...
ICE?

Ísafjarðarbær

Húnaflói

Skagafjörður

Breiðafjörður

Blönduló

Stykkishólmur

Snæfellsjökull

ICELAND VOLCANO
The highest concentration of active volcanoes outside of the Ring of Fire can be found in Iceland! With more than 30 volcanic systems, Iceland's volcanoes have spewed a third of the Earth's total **lava** output over the past 500 years!

Keflavík

In 2010, one "minor" eruption sent a plume of volcanic ash into the air that halted air travel in northern Europe for several weeks.

Tindfjalla-jökull

Eyjafjalla-jökull

Mýr jö

Vestmannaeyjar

Heimaey

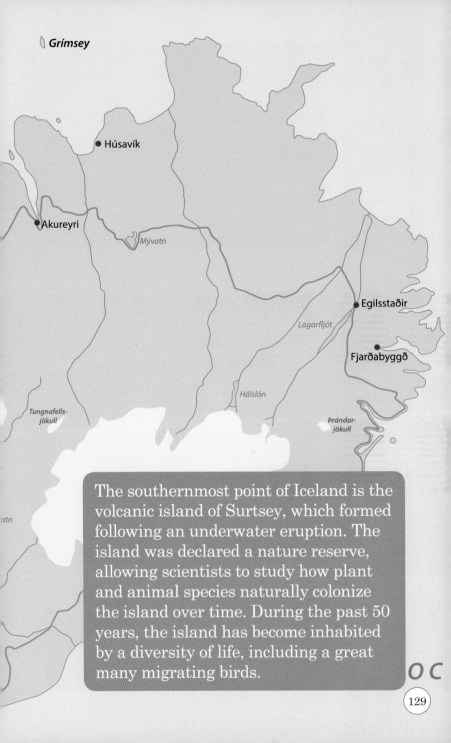

Grímsey

● Húsavík

● Akureyri

Mývatn

● Egilsstaðir

Lagarfljót

● Fjarðabyggð

Hálslón

*Tungnafells-
jökull*

*Þrándar-
jökull*

atn

The southernmost point of Iceland is the
volcanic island of Surtsey, which formed
following an underwater eruption. The
island was declared a nature reserve,
allowing scientists to study how plant
and animal species naturally colonize
the island over time. During the past 50
years, the island has become inhabited
by a diversity of life, including a great
many migrating birds.

O C

RAIN FORESTS

Forests that are characterized by large amounts of rain (no less than 66 inches annually) are called **rain forests**. Most are **tropical** rain forests and are located near the **Equator**, though temperate rain forests can be found in milder climates scattered throughout the world.

RAIN FORESTS HAVE 4 LAYERS

an emergent layer, where the tallest trees break through

a high **canopy** of collective treetops

an understory, above the ground but below most tree leaves

a forest floor at ground level

By some estimates, half of all plant species and a quarter of all insect species live in the canopy, high up off the ground!

TRUE OR FALSE?
These lush areas are sometimes called jewels of the Earth because of how valuable they are to the world as a whole.

CHALLENGE YOURSELF!

ANSWER: True! Believed to be the oldest **ecosystems** on Earth, rain forests are home to more than half of the world's known species of plants and animals, with millions of others still undiscovered.

There are islands shaped like half-moons, hearts, smiley faces, cartoon characters, boomerangs, and various animals (including dolphins, stingrays, and sea horses). But perhaps the most unusually shaped islands on Earth are found in an equally unlikely place: at the edge of the Arabian Desert!

Dubai, in the United Arab Emirates, is home to some of the most striking man-made islands in the world.

STRANGE SHAPES!

THE WORLD ISLANDS, DUBAI

The World Islands development project consists of 300 private islands, forming the shape of a global map when viewed from above. Even though only two of the islands have been developed, as a result of the 2008 world financial crisis, with the remaining uninhabited islands left only as sand, the **archipelago** remains a sight to behold from the air.

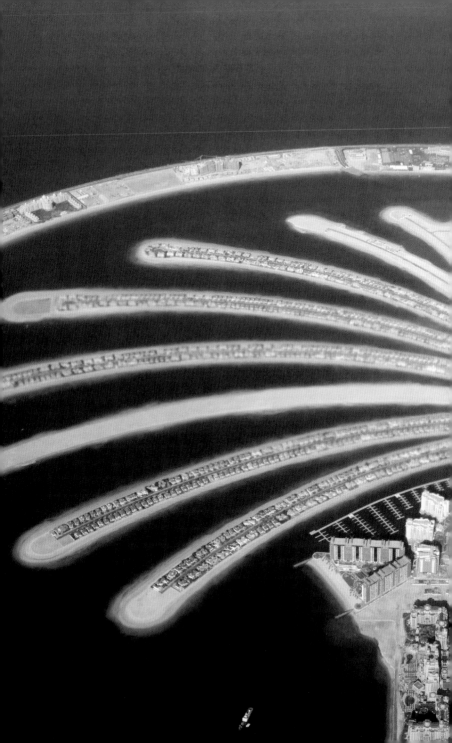

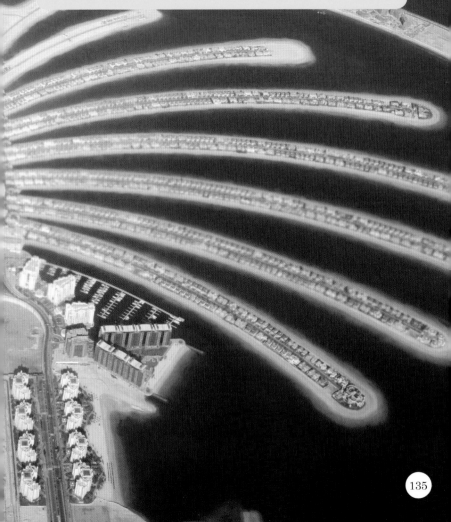

THE PALM, DUBAI

Made entirely of dredged sand and rocks, the Palm Islands took 5 years to construct. The result was a 323-mile stretch of palm-shaped beach that serves as residential and entertainment space. The Prince of Dubai himself conceived of the idea, hoping to increase tourism in the area.

Water in the world's oceans is always moving. **Tides** cause water levels to rise and fall. Other vast movements within the ocean, called **currents**, cause water to flow from one place to another. These currents are caused by wind, as well as by differences in water temperature and saltiness of the water.

Did you know that the moon is responsible for most of the movement of the tides? The moon is so big that its gravity actually pulls at the Earth's water! The oceans swell as the moon passes above each night. The rotation of the Earth itself and the sun's gravity are factors, too, but nothing has more of an impact on tidal levels than the moon.

Ocean currents
are responsible for heating and cooling the wind and, therefore, the air on land.

BORNEO

The **rain forest** on the island of Borneo in Southeast Asia is at least 140 million years old—it was around before the extinction of the dinosaurs! Considered the last great rain forest of Asia, it is believed to be the oldest forest in the world!

The Borneo rain forest is roughly the size of the U.S. state of California, and yet it's home to 6% of the entire world's **biodiversity**! Among these animals are several vulnerable endangered species, such as pygmy elephants, orangutans, Borneo rhinoceroses, proboscis monkeys, clouded leopards, and sun bears.

We shot the first season of *Survivor* on the island of Borneo—over 15 years ago. It was really lush and full of monitor lizards and snakes! We lived in tents, and I could hear them just outside of where I slept each night!

There are two main types of natural islands: **continental islands** and **oceanic islands**.

Oceanic islands are formed by underwater volcanoes! Eruptions on the seafloor cause layers of **lava** to build up. Sometimes, the resulting mound of rock breaks the surface of the water, forming new land above **sea level**.

The Hawaiian Islands, which make up the 50th and most recent state in the United States, formed this way. In fact, islands continue to form! All of them were formed by the same underwater **magma** source, called a **hot spot**, which remains active today.

The newest volcano in Hawaii's **archipelago**, or island chain, is named Lōʻihi. It lies 22 miles off the coast of the Big Island. Though Lōʻihi hasn't erupted since 1996, it might erupt again someday— potentially forming a new Hawaiian Island.

Underwater hot spots don't move, but the vast Pacific plate on which all of the islands stand does. As the plate moves slowly above the hot spot, individual islands form. The theory behind this very large-scale movement of the Earth's **crust** is called **plate tectonics**.

BORN FROM VOLCANOES

LAKE TITICACA

The largest lake in South America, Lake Titicaca is also the highest navigable lake in the world! It is nestled in the Andes Mountains on the border of Peru and Bolivia, and the surface of Lake Titicaca is an amazing 12,507 feet above **sea level**.

CRAZY BUT TRUE

The **basin** of Lake Titicaca formed about 60 million years ago, when unthinkably powerful earthquakes broke the Andes Mountain range into two pieces! After the Ice Age, melting glacier water gathered in the hollows left behind, creating lakes and rivers high up in the mountains.

SPOTTED LAKE

Considered a sacred site by the First Nations of the Okanagan Valley, Canada's Spotted Lake becomes a colorful spectacle every summer. Mineral deposits crystallize as the nutrient-rich water evaporates, forming "spots" of green, blue, white, and yellow.

PINK LAKE

There are a number of lakes throughout the world that have naturally pink salt water! One such lake in Western Australia turns pink every summer when special algae build up in the water. Some people say the color resembles a strawberry milkshake!

There are different ways to measure bodies of water. Scientists regularly measure the **surface area**, **volume**, and depth of the world's lakes over time to determine their average sizes.

- Surface area describes the size of a lake as it appears flat on a map.
- Volume describes how much water a lake holds.
- Depth describes how deep the lake floor is from the surface of the water.

LAKE SUPERIOR

The largest lake in the world by surface area is Lake Superior in North America. It covers an area of

31,700 square miles.

LAKE BAIKAL

The largest lake in the world by volume is Lake Baikal in Russia. It holds 5,700 cubic miles of water. That's more than 6.25 quadrillion gallons!

That's 20% of the world's total surface freshwater!

Lake Baikal is also the deepest lake in the world, with a maximum depth of 5,387 feet.

Lake Baikal freezes, despite being the world's deepest lake. Every year, the ice that forms on Lake Baikal's surface is thick enough for cars to drive across it! The lake is also home to hundreds of species of animals, including the world's only population of freshwater seals.

MONURIKI ISLAND, FIJI

Islands with no people living on them are called **desert islands**. One such island is named Monuriki Island. Part of the Mamanuca Island group in Fiji, the uninhabited island has become a popular tourist destination since 2000, when it was featured in the film *Cast Away*, starring Tom Hanks.

NI'IHAU, HAWAII

Nicknamed the Forbidden Isle, Ni'ihau has been privately owned since 1864. With an area of 69.5 square miles, the westernmost of the Hawaiian Islands has been closed to most visitors since 1915. Nearly all of the island's 130 permanent inhabitants are Native Hawaiians.

EASTER ISLAND

A Polynesian island in the south-eastern Pacific Ocean, Easter Island is famous for its giant stone statues of human heads. Called *moai* by the native islanders, each weighs as much as 14 tons! There are 887 *moai* on the island, and the specifics of their origin remain somewhat mysterious.

HOT SPRINGS

Iceland is home to many hot springs, which are powered by underground volcanoes! When groundwater is heated by magma-heated rocks, it rises, mixing with surface water.

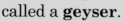

ERUPTIONS OF WATER!

Sometimes, boiling water gets trapped, producing a great deal of energy. When it finally escapes, the water can shoot high into the air, forming what's called a **geyser**.

GREAT GEYSIR

Perhaps Iceland's most popular natural attraction is the Great Geysir, an eruption of water that is so famous all other geysers in the world were named after it! Iceland's Geysir can shoot scalding water higher than a 20-story building!

DEEP-SEA GEYSERS

Not all geysers are on land! Deep under the ocean surface, fissures at the seafloor called hydrothermal vents release plumes of super-heated water. The vents provide energy and food for a host of deep-sea life-forms, including bacteria, clams, and tube worms.

HOW HOT IS LAVA?

Lava is the name for **magma** after it's separated from the Earth's interior.

As hot and dangerous as lava is, Earth's most disastrous eruptions were more deadly for the amount of **tephra** and gases expelled into the atmosphere than from lava flows alone. Tephra includes ash and debris that pose a threat not only to the region around a volcano but to the entire world, causing global climate change and even mass extinctions.

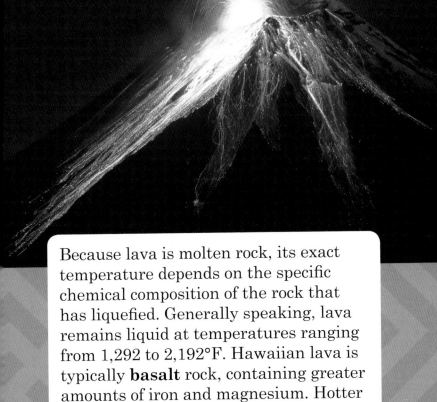

Because lava is molten rock, its exact temperature depends on the specific chemical composition of the rock that has liquefied. Generally speaking, lava remains liquid at temperatures ranging from 1,292 to 2,192°F. Hawaiian lava is typically **basalt** rock, containing greater amounts of iron and magnesium. Hotter than other lava, it flows at a range of 1,832 to 2,282°F! It's so hot that even the air coming off it can burn you!

CRAZY BUT TRUE

Lava is 100,000 times as viscous as water, meaning it is thicker as a liquid! Being more viscous allows lava to flow for a long time before cooling. It even flows underwater!

MOUNT EVEREST

Mount Everest, the tallest mountain in the world, with a peak 29,035 feet above sea level, is also the most isolated summit. The closest of its neighboring peaks is almost 25,000 feet away!

CRAZY BUT TRUE

The very peak of Mount Everest is made of "marine limestone"! According to the nonfiction writer John McPhee, the rock that forms much of the summit is composed of the skeletal remains of prehistoric sea creatures. There is evidence that the same rock lifted up by the pushing of **tectonic plates** was once as much as 20,000 feet below the seafloor. Talk about from one extreme to the other!

Located in the Himalayas, on the border between China and Nepal, Mount Everest is more than 60 million years old. It was formed by two **tectonic plates** pushing up against each other over time! And, believe it or not, the mountain continues to grow— by about a quarter of an inch every year!

The island nation of Japan was born from a volcanic **hot spot**. Japan's islands stand on some of the most active volcanoes in the world. More than 30 islands directly south of Tokyo, Japan, make up the Bonin Islands **archipelago**.

BORN NOVEMBER 20, 2013

Having first formed 48 million years ago, islands in the Bonin chain are still appearing. In fact, a new island broke the surface of the Pacific Ocean in 2013! Within months, the small island grew so big that it merged with the neighboring island of Nishinoshima. Together, they have formed a new landmass 3,280 feet across!

MAP OF JAPAN

OTHER NEWBORN ISLANDS

Born September 24, 2013:
Zalzala Koh is the name of a new island that formed off the coast of Gwadar in Balochistan, Pakistan. It measures roughly 575 by 525 feet.

Born October 30, 2013:
A new island named Principato di San Bernardino is now part of the Zubair Islands, a group of 10 islands off the west coast of Yemen, in the Arabian Peninsula. It measures 1,700 by 2,300 feet.

The average depth of the world's oceans is nearly 3 miles! If you rode a standard elevator that far down without stopping, it would take you more than half an hour!

But the deepest part of the world's oceans is in the Mariana Trench, in the western Pacific Ocean. It reaches a maximum depth of 36,840 feet. That's more than 6.8 miles under the surface of the ocean!

Mount Everest is the highest point on Earth. But what is the lowest? A trench deep in the ocean floor!

CRAZY BUT TRUE

Mount Everest could fit in the Mariana Trench, with 6,805 feet to spare!

GLOSSARY

AIR TEMPERATURE: A degree of hotness or coldness of the air as measured by a thermometer.

ARCHIPELAGO: A group of islands close together.

BASALT: A common type of dark volcanic rock made mainly of silica and oxygen.

BASIN: A large, bowl-shaped depression in a landscape.

BIODIVERSITY: The variety of species found in one place.

BIOME: Region of the world with common ecological characteristics, such as climate and weather.

BOREAL FOREST: A northern forest with a great number of coniferous trees, such as pine and fir trees.

CANOPY: A forest layer consisting of overlapping treetops.

COASTAL DESERT: A complex desert system found on the western coasts of continents and characterized by low rainfall due to cold, dry winds.

COLD DESERT: A dry region where extremely cold air temperatures limit rainfall and other precipitation.

CONTINENTAL ISLAND: An island formed by land that split off from a larger continent.

CRUST: Earth's outermost layer of solid rock.

CURRENT: A continuous flow of moving water, like a river moving within an ocean.

DESERT: A biome characterized by extremely dry climates.

DESERT ISLAND: An isolated island with few or no people living on it.

ECOSYSTEM: A community of living organisms and their environment interacting as a system.

EQUATOR: An imaginary circle around the Earth exactly halfway between the North and South Poles.

EROSION: The eating away of rock or soil by wind and water.

ESTUARY: A partially enclosed body of water, where fresh-water mixes with salt water.

FOSSIL: The preserved remains or impressions of a once-living organism, such as a plant or an animal.

FUMAROLE: A vent in the Earth's crust where volcanic gases escape into the air.

GEYSER: An explosive jet of heated water released from within the Earth.

GRASSLAND: A biome dominated by various types of grasses and few or no trees.

HOT SPOT: An underwater volcanic magma source.

HYDRIC SOIL: Wetland soil characterized by excessive moisture.

IGNEOUS ROCK: Rock formed from cooled molten rock.

INLAND SEA: A shallow sea found within a landmass.

LAND TEMPERATURE: A degree of hotness or coldness of the surface of the ground as measured by satellite technology.

LAVA: Magma that has reached the Earth's surface following volcanic eruption.

LAVA TUBE: A hollow tunnel formed by a lava flow, in which the outermost rock cools while the still-molten center drains away.

MAGMA: Molten rock beneath the Earth's surface.

MID-OCEAN RIDGE: A long, underwater mountain system where new oceanic crust forms.

NORTHERN HEMISPHERE: The half of the Earth that is north of the Equator.

OCEANIC ISLAND: An island formed by an underwater volcano.

PETRIFIED WOOD: A type of fossil in which the organic tissues of trees have been slowly replaced by minerals.

PLATE TECTONICS: The theory that plates of crust that form the Earth's surface are slowly moving and interacting.

POLAR DESERT: The cold desert found specifically at one of the Earth's two poles.

PRECIPITATION: The general name for water falling from clouds, such as rain or snow, regardless of what form it takes.

RAIN FOREST: Dense, wet forests containing great biodiversity.

SEA LEVEL: The height of the ocean's surface, from which elevation is measured.

SPELEOLOGY: The study of caves.

SPELUNKING: The activity of exploring caves.

STALACTITE: A hanging rock formation, like an icicle, made of hardened minerals.

STALAGMITE: A cone-shaped rock formation coming up from the floor of a cave, resembling an upside-down stalactite.

SURFACE AREA: The mathematical measure of the total surface of something.

TECTONIC PLATE: An individual slab of rock that forms the surface skin of the Earth.

TEPHRA: The debris and ash expelled from a volcanic explosion.

TIDE: The rise and fall of the Earth's surface water.

TOPOGRAPHIC MAP: A type of map that uses lines and shading to show natural and man-made features, such as elevation.

TROPICAL: Located within the region called the tropics.

TROPICS: The region of the Earth surrounding the Equator.

TUNDRA: A cold and treeless biome characteristic of arctic and subarctic regions.

VOLUME: The amount of space contained within something.

WETLAND: A biome characterized by water-saturated land or the plants and animals adapted to live in saturated conditions.

INDEX